I0213448

# <u>*No Excuse!*</u> Selling

## Why did you get into the sales business anyway?

## By
## Robert Kennedy

Copyright © 2012 Robert Kennedy

All rights reserved. No part of this publication may be reproduced, stored in a retrieval system, or transmitted in any form or by any means, electronic, mechanical, recording, or otherwise, without the prior written permission of the author.

Printed in the United States of America.

ISBN-10: 1622980017
ISBN-13: 9781622980017

**To all the professionals who strive to improve themselves in order to earn an extra dollar!**

# _Table of Contents_

# Introduction

*"I do not believe in excuses. I believe in hard work as the prime solvent of life's problems."*
~ *James Cash Penny*

*"NO EXCUSE!!!"* It's a mindset that any type of executive needs to maintain as it is the KEY to success or failure. In a sales environment, there really is nothing more important than the mindset of *"No Excuse!"* All too often in the process of developing a sales career, many fall into the trap of patting themselves on the back and celebrating their greatness when things are going well. However, when the inevitable "down swing" in a sales career arises, people are equally quick to blame everyone and everything around them for their lack of success.

DO... NOT... DO IT! There is *No Excuse!*

The mindset of *"No Excuse!"* might mean something slightly different depending on where you are in your sales career. If you're early in your career, you may not have had the experience of a prolonged stall in your sales performance, which will make this book your guide to what you need to avoid. You may be a more seasoned sales executive who has lost sight of the things that have gotten you where you are today. If so, this book is going to be an excellent reminder of what you may already know but have moved away from. In either case, this will be your guide as long as you remember that what you're going through is nothing new to seasoned sales people. The "trick" is to remember the core principles of successful sales people, learn from them, and get back to what you're good at.

Now, let's take a very introspective look at yourself and your situation. Are you justifying failure or poor performance on things that you like to call "reasons," which are in fact simple "excuses?"
Have you found yourself saying things like the following?

- "I wasn't feeling well, so I didn't do well last week."

- "That new guy they hired is stealing all the good leads!"

- "That last client was a jerk... that's why he didn't sign the contract."

Think hard and answer this question honestly: "Have I been making excuses?" This behavior can go on and on forever. If you try hard enough, you'll talk yourself into the "reason" that you didn't get the sale was because your client had blue eyes and you have brown eyes, so they didn't like you. I've said it before, and it's time to say it again...

DO... NOT... DO IT!

What it boils down to is that you KNEW what the job was about when you took it. You knew the expectations. You understood that pressure to produce is a fact of selling, and you understood what it was going to take to become a success. For a time, you may have achieved a strong understanding of this and transferred it into an advantage for yourself. Now you find that excuses are creeping into your psyche and affecting your performance.

IT IS TIME to push them aside, step up to the plate, and accept personal responsibility for your performance. It is time to become the sales professional that you're meant to be and that deep down you know that you are! Take the right steps to get the training you need. Blame no one but yourself when things aren't going well. Turn iron into GOLD, and always remember that your career is what you make it—now and forever. You, and ONLY you, are responsible for where your career goes, so start today—right here, right now!

Have I scared you off yet? Well, if you got this far, you've already committed to taking those steps. The goal of this book is to help you understand some harsh realities about the sales environment that you either have yet to be exposed to or you may have forgotten. The goal is also to get you fired up about sales and your sales career—not by giving you "rah-rah" speeches, but by giving you guidance and the benefit of experience. It's to provide you with key components to success that you may not have heard before. It's to remind you of those key principles which have brought you to where you are today that may have been lost in the hectic pace of your environment or simply because you've developed some bad habits! Any successful sales executive already understands that there are certain core ideas that MUST be incorporated into their daily routine— and that's what this book will help you with.

Anyone can learn the skills to successful selling. There are countless books, seminars, articles, and opinions about how to effectively sell. If you've done your research, by now, you've probably found a dozen different acronyms that you are told, "if you follow these, you'll be a success!" Not to take away from these techniques—they do have value—but I would like to demonstrate throughout this book how your "mindset" will lead to your success or failure. The time is NOW to set yourself up for success. It's about what you do, not what you didn't do...No *Excuse!*

What exactly does "*No Excuse* Selling," mean? Well, the answer depends on your goals and aspirations, doesn't it? You may not strive to be the top salesperson on the planet who is able to sell ice to Eskimos, but you certainly don't want to be the person listed at the bottom of every sales report either! What's important is that you need to recognize and view the sales profession for what it is at its core: to influence and guide someone to make a decision. This doesn't always mean getting a "yes." A "no" is still a decision. However, you must have the skill, ability, and mindset to guide a person to their decision.

Whether your product is selling make-up, donuts, or a billion dollar airplane or your service is haircuts, house painting, or convincing your friends to get pepperoni on the pizza you're ordering, the pressure to produce results is a fact of selling. No matter what it is, you will have periods of great, soaring success and periods of soul-crushing defeats.

Through it all, you need to remember to *Pursue Your Passion!* Think back to when you first started your career and the hopes, dreams, and expectations you had. Now is NOT the time to drop the torch! Yes, the sales universe has its downsides: fierce competition, significant barriers to entry, lack of direction, etc. But always remember, "Money follows passion." It's never the other way around.

At the end of the day, success or failure in any sales environment boils down to a simple truth: Your "mindset" determines your fate.

Now, let's get started...

# *CHAPTER 1: Delivery*

*"You must be very patient, very persistent. The world isn't going to shower gold coins on you just because you have a good idea. You're going to have to work like crazy to bring that idea to the attention of people. They're not going to buy it unless they know about it."*

~ Herb Kelleher

Before the sales process even begins, you need to be certain that you can deliver on the promises you're about to make to your prospect. Your goal is, of course, to sell to them. When you do, you will have to be able to deliver on the product or service as well as the promises you've made. This is why we will cover a few key points so that you can be certain that your mindset is such that you'll be able to deliver effectively.

But before we do that, a question:

**?** *No Excuse!* Question #1:
*What do you really want... clients or customers?*

> ➤ Answer: You always want CLIENTS! What is the difference? It's simple: Customers buy *from* you. Clients buy *into* you!

That may sound like clever word play, but let's give that some thought for a moment. When you look at your book of business, based on the definition above, how many clients do you have and how many customers do you have? The person whom calls you to place their order, are they calling you because they happen to have your number? Is it a quick, no-nonsense transaction that anyone (including your competitor) can do for them? Or are they calling you because you've taken the time to understand their needs?

Perhaps it's because you've recently reached out to them to make sure everything is going well, and it prompted them to call you to place their order.  The difference often separates the successful sales person from those that are squeaking by.

Make no mistake; whether this is a person with whom you have a long-standing relationship or it's someone you just met, whether it's a "client" or a "customer," they are all "prospects" when the sales cycle begins.  If your product or service is a simple commodity or a complex transaction, the prospect has a decision to make: to call you or to call someone else.  Of course, you certainly increase your chances of success if it's a "client" making the decision, because you've proven in the past that you add value above and beyond the purchase.  So how do you effectively turn customers into clients, and how do you keep clients happy?

❖ *No Excuse!* Action Item That Works #1:
  *Personal follow up works!*

> The last time you wrapped up a deal and the sale was over, what did you do?  Did you mark the sale on your report, pat yourself on the back, and move on to the next one?  When things get busy and the pressure for performance is high, it's often easy to forget that the person who you just sold to is your bread and butter.  If you want them to return as a "client," you will want to remember to acknowledge them by thanking them for their business, letting them know that you understand that they have a choice and you're thankful they decided to buy from you.

A simple idea (basic, but easily forgotten in the hectic world of sales) is to send a *personalized* thank you note or e-mail. Another idea is to post a public social media posting thanking them for their business. Yes, Facebook and Twitter can be used for something other than letting people know what you had for dinner! A restaurant gift card, tickets to a baseball game, anything that will let your client know you appreciate them and their business is always a great idea. They will remember the thank you, and they'll remember whom it came from. Doesn't that set you up nicely for the next time?

## ☀ Don't #1: *Don't "oversell" and "under deliver."*

Let's begin with the concept of "overselling and under-delivering." Overselling is simply the "art" of puffing up your product or service as the greatest thing since sliced bread, when in fact it may be a commodity. It's all well and good to highlight the features of your product or why your service is better than the competition across the street; that's good sales. But over-doing it to build interest will only lead to problems if you can't deliver on those grandiose claims!

It's also the "art" of convincing a prospective client that you can accomplish or deliver more than what you really can. Not only does your product or service need to deliver, but also so do you. Your client will have expectations of service and quality that you need to be certain you can live up to. When you over promise and under deliver, you risk damage to your credibility that will be difficult, and sometimes impossible, to win back!

Learn to put yourself in a position of "over delivering," which will never leave you holding the short end of the stick and having to explain why the things you promised can't be delivered. Who was an expert at this? Scotty on the *Enterprise*, of course! Did you ever notice how he was always able to get things fixed in less time than what he told Captain Kirk it would take? You can never go wrong when you exceed expectations, as long as you don't wear a red shirt, which as we know didn't always end well on *Star Trek.*

An excellent quote by Jack Canfield, the author of *The Success Principles*, sums it up well by stating, "If you want to really excel at what you do—really become a howling success in school, business, or life—do more than what is required, always giving something extra, something that is not expected. A business that goes the extra mile earns the respect, loyalty, and referrals of its customers."

Let's take this and apply it to a few common, real world examples...

*Example #1: You sell cars at a dealership,* and you are approached by a nice couple whose primary concern is economy and fuel mileage. They've just told you that they looked at the same vehicle across the street and were told that the car gets 27 miles per gallon. Knowing that the competition across the street has already spoken with them, you're anxious to prove that they should buy from you, so you blurt out, "Actually, I've been told by other owners of this same car that they're seeing 35 miles per gallon!" This isn't a fabrication; you've actually been told this. The problem is that the sales person across the street pulled out the official MPG guide that says 27 miles per gallon. So, how are you going to explain that?

Although you may have felt that you were telling them what they wanted to hear, you may have just blown the opportunity by over-promising something. Even if they buy from you, you run the risk that they'll be back in three months wondering why they aren't getting 35 miles per gallon, like you said. Word of mouth spreads, and the dealership across the street gets the business.

*Example #2: You sell meat to restaurants.* It's your job to get restaurant owners to buy the meat that your company sells to serve in their establishments. In order to secure sales, you start promising pricing that convinces them that you are the right choice. You've now returned to your office to write up the deal, only to find that your supervisor says, "There's no way we can do it for that price!" Now what do you do?

How do you avoid such pitfalls? For starters, stick to the basics. This sounds simple enough, but it's something that's easily forgotten. Sticking with the basics is the best path to creating sustainable sales.

Overselling (leading to under delivering) also occurs when your sales process begins going above and beyond what you normally do! You may have your sales pitch down pat, worked the same thing successfully over and over, but then, you run into a client that won't make their buying decision immediately! If you've found yourself jumping into panic mode thinking, *I didn't do my presentation right!,* then you've opened the door to overselling.

Have you caught yourself pushing the benefits of your product or service even after the buying decision has been made? If the buying decision hasn't been made, have you found yourself trying to convince your prospect to go with you by bad-mouthing your competition? What about continually reassuring the buyer that they're making the right decision by going with you, rather than letting them come to their own conclusions?  What about "justification?" Have you found yourself justifying certain components of your product or service in an effort to convince your prospect to buy?  All of these traps lead to overselling.  If you've followed your sales pitch, the one that has worked countless times in the past, ask yourself why you think more is necessary! You may simply have a customer that doesn't WANT to buy from you, which is ok.  It's when you start making promises that you can't deliver that the real problems begin.

❖ *No Excuse!* Action Item That Works #2:
   *Follow a routine!*

> The "basics" can be better adhered to when you remember to follow a routine that works.  You're familiar with this phrase: "If it ain't broke, don't fix it." Successful sales people will continually tweak and adjust their sales pitch to see if there is a better way to do things, but the basic "process" doesn't change. There isn't a golfer in the world from Tiger Woods to Jim-the-Hacker who just launched his ball into the parking lot that hasn't worked on their swing. Unfortunately, a trap to fall into is when it works once or twice, and suddenly, that's the way to go!  In fact, it's the analysis over the long term that determines if a technique, phrase, or style is effective.

> When in doubt, make sure you follow a standard routine, tailored to the situation and the client, with subtle changes.  This is true for any point within the sales process, from pre-work to the follow up thank you.  Again, sales is a "process," and a routine will help to keep you on the path that's worked in the past and will work in the future.

You also have to understand your *limitations*—both with yourself and with your product. Don't promise that you can complete something in 3 days when in fact it will take 5. Don't promise that your pricing will ALWAYS be lower if you can't back it up. Don't tout skills that you don't have!

Of course, you may do these things well and still run into issues. This is where, as a salesperson, your follow through will make or break your career. More importantly is what you learn from these situations and how you prevent them from happening again. As Dale Carnegie once stated, "The successful man will profit from his mistakes and try again in a different way." In short, you will be faced with these challenges, but you MUST learn from them or be doomed to repeat your mistakes.

When it comes to working through issues, resulting from over promising and under delivering, a basic tenant is that no one likes surprises. What people like even less is a lack of communication! You find that a promised delivery date will be delayed, and you have the option of contacting your client to let them know or crossing your fingers and hoping things work out ok. It may be an uncomfortable phone call, but you need to follow through with your clients so that they know to expect something different. That's how trust is built in the client/salesperson relationship.

We've all run into this and have to work through it. This is exactly why, if you want to be a professional, successful sales person, you have to be sure that you're never caught off guard!

💣 Don't #2: *Don't be caught off guard!*

Of course, as time goes by, you will understand processes and procedures within your organization better. This will lead you to more prepared and polished sales presentations to your potential clients that will help you avoid those pitfalls. However, there's another key component that will vary from day to day: your customers!

If you've watched successful sales people deal with clients, you might sometimes be amazed at how smoothly they interact and how they seem to understand what a client will want before they client even knows what they want. These successful sales people have learned that you must know your customer.

Over time, you will learn your customers' likes and dislikes. You'll learn about their hobbies, interests, family and friends. In short, you will be able to relate to them better. This is extremely important, because buying is not only based on the product or service you offer. It's also based on the level of service you provide. A good analogy to remember is that employees of a company don't quit the "company," they quit the people that they work with. The same holds true for client relationships: If they don't like you, they'll go with someone else.

❖ *No Excuse!* Action Item That Works #3:
   *Remain consistent!*

> Implement consistency, not only as it relates to learning more about your client, but also as it relates to all aspects of a successful sales cycle—from understanding your industry and/or product better to your process in dealing with clients to your routine for

following up with prospects or recent sales. Consistency is Key!

When you develop the mentality and habits that have led you to success, do not abandon them! Consistently learning about each client, about your competitors, and about your company; this is second nature to successful sales people. Those that look for short cuts, the easy way out, and the faster way to short-term success inevitably end up with an inconsistent approach to their career and their performance will suffer.

A very basic example: *you're a successful salesman* in the middle of a record year. For years you arrived at the office at 5 a.m., worked for hours, worked closely with your team, and mapped out goals to improve your weaknesses. You've always been consistent in sales, and you think everything is going great. So, maybe you can roll in at 7 a.m. from now on. Will your performance suffer because of a short cut? Absolutely! DO NOT let this happen in your own career; it will happen faster than you think!

To prove that this is a truth, ask one of your clients if they've ever paid more for a product or service because they liked the sales person they were dealing with. Ask them if they've ever followed a sales person from one company to another. Ask them who the is the first person they go to for their various needs—be it banking, furniture, copiers, cars, etc. This should demonstrate beyond a doubt how important it is to understand their needs, all the while remembering. "If you're the last to know, you're the first to go!"

It may be an attractive concept: Find a short cut, and you can spend more time on something else. The problem is this: You're talking yourself into creating short cuts to your own sales career!  Who is the one who suffers?  Not your competition, that's for sure, and not the sales person who's practicing a consistent routine for their own success. In fact, they wouldn't mind you failing one bit!  Who suffers is your client, which in turn affects you when they aren't calling you when that next opportunity arises.

💣※ Don't #3: *Don't be "that" guy!*

When it comes to delivering, you certainly don't want to turn into "that guy."  We've all heard the stories from clients: "That guy never calls me back." "That guy doesn't know what he's talking about." "I'll never deal with that guy again."  Becoming "that guy" is easier than you might think, but not as hard to avoid as you might think.

Additionally, getting yourself out from under the label of "that guy" is a nearly impossible task.  This "designation" doesn't happen overnight.  We all have made a bonehead mistake now and again that has cost us a deal or a relationship.  We've all said something that we didn't mean to say, let something slip through the cracks, or simply "flaked" out on something.  Look back on your career so far, and I'm sure you will be able to recall an instance that you now say, "Oh, wow! How did that ever happen!?"  If you're lucky, you've learned from those mistakes and never repeated them, where you're now able to look back and laugh.

Others, however, take a different approach.  Have you ever heard someone lose a sale because of an easily avoidable mistake and proclaim, "Big deal, it's only one customer?"  Maybe you've heard "Oh, I'm not going to let him know his shipment will be late; I think he's a jerk."  I bet you've heard, "Oops, I guess I forgot to give them a call." These are all classic signs of someone who doesn't care if they become "that guy."

People like this let occurrence after occurrence pile up until the mound of "individual examples" becomes so great that they couldn't climb the pile without a Sherpa guide. That's when "that guy" is born. Customers stop calling, sales performance plummets, and they can be heard to say (to quote Homer Simpson), "Why do things that happen to stupid people keep happening to me???"

That's a simple answer to anyone who is paying attention. When you are overselling and under delivering, when you're constantly being surprised by problems during the sales process, it all leads to mistakes and a reputation that is tough to avoid. The damage control that is required to erase this black cloud is enormous. Always be aware of this throughout your sales career. You'll see others around you who have become "that guy," but it's what you want to avoid.

Avoiding it is actually straightforward, but again, sometimes it's easy to forget. The core value to remember here is to let your hard work dictate your value to your clients. Your customers are intelligent people, and they can see right through smoke screens. The really intelligent ones will allow you to think that it's working when in fact they're busy behind the scenes getting ready to dump you and your company!

✖ *No Excuse!* Salesology Principle #1:
*If you do well or if you do badly, you're going to reap what you sow. Take personal responsibility, and hold yourself to a higher standard!*

When you start cutting corners, not putting in the effort, not following through, your performance will suffer. When the extra effort, attention to details, and learning from your failures becomes a chore, it will be no time until you start reaping the results. Those that succeed strive for top performance every day. Those that under perform strive for... well, very little... and it shows in their results.

Let me share a story of two high school buddies of mine: One was voted most likely to succeed, and the other was written off and was expected to accomplish nothing. The "most likely to succeed" friend of mine got lazy and wound up in a mediocre, dead-end job. The underestimated buddy of mine worked every day like it was his last, and he is now the owner of 4 car lots. We laughed when recalling the label he carried around in high school, but in the end, he had the last laugh because he didn't let laziness get in the way of his success.

The point of this is simple: Hard work breeds success, while laziness breeds... nothing. When you find yourself cutting corners, making excuses to avoid getting things done, or putting in that extra effort, you will reap what you sow. Your clients will see the work you put in, as will your co-workers, managers, and family. The long-term rewards to be achieved by going that extra mile far outweigh the temporary short-term joy of leaving work early one day to go golfing. When you forget that your goal is to be a success in the field of sales, you begin down this path, and it affects everything around you—including the career you've been working so hard to build.

# CHAPTER 2: Expectation Management

*"Experience taught me a few things. One is to listen to your gut no matter how good something sounds on paper. The second is that you are generally better off sticking with what you know and the third is that sometimes, your best investments are the ones you don't make."*

~ Donald Trump

Let's jump deeper into the concept of "*No Excuse* Selling" with a detailed discussion about expectations. What is the first thing that pops into your mind when the term "expectation management" is used? Do you begin thinking of your personal expectations you've set for yourself in your personal and work life? Do you think about the expectations that your clients and prospects place on you? Do you think about the goals and responsibilities that your company has placed upon your shoulders as part of your sales position? Or, maybe your mind creates a montage of all three that begins to feel a bit overwhelming!

Of course, the sales universe encompasses all three, and all three are constantly pulling you in different directions. At the end of the day, you will find that how you handle these expectations will be a key measure of your success! From a personal perspective, achieving realistic goals and moving forward with the things that are important in your own life will affect how you perceive yourself. From a client perspective, well-handled expectations will affect the perception they have toward you. From the viewpoint of your company, it will affect how they view your performance, which often times, can be a very subjective view. Beyond the "perceptions," expectations will drive all of your actions and decisions!

What does this tell us? It tells us that a lack of focus on expectation management will inevitably result in a slow spiral into confusion and failure. If this occurs, who is to blame? Well, if you've understood the concepts presenting in this book so far, your only answer will be "I'm the only one to blame." Everything circles back to the mindset of "*No Excuse!* Selling," and this chapter is designed to help you through the sometimes-daunting task of managing all of the expectations that are put upon you.

This chapter will dig deeper into the three major segments of expectation management: personal, client, and company. It will deliver a framework for you to follow that includes the following: setting appropriate and manageable expectations, monitoring and measuring these expectations, and finally influencing the expectations of each group successfully.

We will discuss the importance of sincerity—not only with yourself, but also with your clients and your organization. We will also discuss the delicate balance that exists between you and your clients, as well as the relationship between you and your company. Also, as part of how one influences their sales world, we will discuss the importance of follow up and follow through.

"The expectations of life depend upon diligence; the mechanic that would perfect his work must first sharpen his tools." Does this not ring true? Does this not apply directly to you and your career? Your tools—knowledge, education, experience, technique, etc.—all must be continually "sharpened" in order to achieve success. It's amazing that a quote from Confucius over 1500 years ago hits so directly to today's sales executives. Keep this in mind today and throughout your career! And always remember that it is YOU that must sharpen your tools. YOU are the one responsible for your career. It's the bad mechanic who expects his assistant to maintain his tools, and it's the bad mechanic who blames his assistant because it wasn't done right.

**?** *No Excuse!* Question #2:
*How did you start your day today?*

> ➤ <u>Answer:</u> The answer you should be saying out loud is this: "I started my day with *NO EXCUSE!*"
>
> If you said that, it means you've been paying attention! Yesterday could have been one of the worst days you've had in months. That huge sale you were anticipating didn't come through. Your boss ripped your head off for something that wasn't even your fault. You stayed up late to finish that proposal, and you're exhausted.
>
> But isn't today a new day? Doesn't today have the possibility to be your best day? YES, it does! As long as you believe it; it does. Get your mindset right, and remove all of the potential obstacles that will keep you from achieving your goals today.
>
> It's the bad quarterback who throws and interception and is afraid to throw that next pass. It's the Hall of Famer who says, "This play is a new play". So why aren't you saying, "This *day* is a new *day,*" and charging forward toward your goals? Get out there, and make THIS day your BEST day!

We are going to use a pretty direct word throughout this chapter, and that word is "lie." When in your personal or business life you find that you are creating expectations that you simply can't manage, you're doing nothing but lying to yourself, your clients, and your company. One might argue that this is a harsh word, that someone could say "over-exaggerated" or "embellished" or "made a mistake." Use whatever phrase you might like, but it all boils down to lying. Unrealistic goals and expectations are nothing more than lies that must be eliminated from your day-to-day life if you ever expect to achieve success.

## ♦※ Don't #1: *Don't lie to YOURSELF*

Let's begin with some introspection. In any professional sales environment, as we've discussed, the first and *only* place to look when it comes to success or failure is yourself. It's also the best place to begin because the easiest person to lie to is yourself. People easily convince themselves that, even though they're 20 pounds overweight, that wolfing down that double cheeseburger deluxe with fries is ok as long as you order a diet soda to go with it. Every day people convince themselves to put off that project (whatever that may be) for one more day because they found something better to do instead.

It's time to pause and reflect on the goals and expectations you set for yourself last month, last year, whenever, and ask yourself if they were realistic. If they were realistic and you didn't reach those goals, then you might be looking for a "reason" that it didn't happen when in fact you're grasping for an "excuse." But what if your goals and aspirations really *were* unrealistic? Does that make it a reason and not an excuse? NO! It's still an excuse; it's just an excuse that you haven't removed from your path. That's what we want to walk through.

First, take the time to set obtainable, realistic goals for yourself! How might you accomplish this? You must be honest with yourself, of course, but you must also take the time and put in the effort to plan, from the end to the beginning. That's right, plan backwards to where you want to go and what you have to do first. Plan how you will step by step meet those goals and how you will work towards the goals you've set.

✖ *No Excuse!* Salesology Principle #2:
   *The early bird gets the worm, but it's the second mouse that gets the cheese!*

> You may also have heard this phrase: "The pioneers get the arrows, while the settlers get the land." Both phrases are equally valid when considering your future plans and how you will achieve them. Careful thought and planning will lead you down the road to success.

When considering setting personal goals and expectations, be sure to incorporate all of the roadblocks that may stand in your way. Are there financial limitations? Do you have the funds available to achieve your goals, or will you have to set intermediate financial goals in order to have the funding needed to reach the end of your path? What about your current skill set? It's possible that you don't have the training or experience today that will help you reach the expectations that you've set for yourself. This might mean that extra time and effort will be required that will need to be considered. Perhaps there simply aren't enough hours in the day for you to complete the tasks! You will need to take the time to plan and organize your days wisely in order to reach the milestones you've set.

Finally, ask yourself "why" you want to set these expectations for yourself! If you wake up one morning and say, "I want to become a professional poker player," and set that as an expectation for yourself without understanding "why" you just said that, you may find that you're not as committed as you thought! Is this a goal because you hate your job? Is it because you want to be famous? Is it because you think you'll make millions? Or is it because you have a passion for poker, and that's the direction you'd like to take your life?

DON'T LIE TO YOURSELF! Personal expectations of any kind are fine, but you need to be honest with yourself about the realities of setting any expectation. Once you do, and you can say to the person looking back at you in the mirror that you know these expectations are realistic and obtainable, and then it's time to get to work on making it happen!

Obviously, setting the goals and expectations are the first step, but now you have to work toward achieving those goals. How exactly are you going to do that? If you've done things properly, you've created steps and milestones that you now have to hold yourself accountable to. If you want to learn how to play guitar, step 1 is... get a guitar! This may require some financial planning, so you'll want to set the milestone of setting aside a certain amount of money so that you can make this purchase. Yes, that's a very basic example, but if you haven't considered that, you'll find yourself six months later saying, "I never learned guitar because I couldn't afford to buy one." Is that a failure? It was a failure—a failure to plan. As mentioned above, serious thought and consideration must be made to the plan in order to achieve success.

- ❖ *No Excuse!* Action Item That Works #4:
  *Be sincere!*

  > Part of successful management of expectations, be it for yourself, your clients, or your company, is "sincerity." In every working relationship, there comes a time when good news and bad news must be delivered. In either case, a sincere delivery of your message done with EMOTION will pay untold dividends. Make the effort to make your communications "human," not clinical or distant. When sincerity is there, trust follows. Lord Byron, English poet of the early 19th century stated, "It is not for minds like ours to give or to receive flatter, yet the praises of sincerity have ever been permitted to the voice of friendship." Our clients, our company, and we ourselves know the difference between flattery and sincerity (or the lack thereof). Use it wisely and see the results!

As with any plan, you need to be sure you are tracking your personal goals and expectations on a regular basis. There are several reasons for doing this, not the least of which is to allow you to motivate yourself because you see progress. The best way to do this is all dependent upon the expectations you've set.

Is a weekly/monthly/quarterly/yearly basis the way to track things? Whichever works best based on the milestones set forth in your plan of attack, be sure to do this on a regular basis to assure consistency and progress.

A better suggestion is to have someone else hold you accountable for the goals you've set. As said earlier, it's easier to lie to yourself than it is to convince someone else of the truth. Again, a person can convince themselves of almost anything if they keep talking themselves into it. If you happen to be one of these people—never really seeming to reach goals and milestones because there's always a "reason"—the time might be right for you to solicit the help of someone else to keep you on task.

Excellent planning and deep soul searching are often the keys to reaching personal goals and fulfilling expectations. However, when it comes to dealing with clients, things might be a bit more straightforward and less complex, but the process is no less important.

### ● Don't #2: *Don't lie to your CLIENTS!*

Now, why would you lie to your clients? It was mentioned before that the word "lie" might seem a little harsh. However, when you've promised more than you can deliver, when the expectations of the client outweigh what you have the ability to provide, you can call it a mistake or omission if you like. Unfortunately, the fact remains that these are "excuses" not "reasons," and you've effectively lied to your clients. Managing expectations is what the core of this chapter is all about.

It begins with an honest assessment of what you can do. You must understand your capabilities and the capabilities of your company and its products or services, and you must deliver this message to your clients clearly and directly. Again, expectations are the primary measure of your success, and in your client's mind, their satisfaction will be measured on how close you come to their expectations.

❖ *No Excuse!* Action Item That Works #5:
  *Understand email etiquette!*

> Every day we need to deal with emails. Most of the
> time, email communication is the best way to
> communicate. It's fast and convenient, and it allows
> you to keep in touch. Unfortunately, when trying to
> use emails to build relationships, they can also be the
> downfall of a sales professional. Although there are
> many pitfalls, such as not properly conveying a
> message or a misinterpretation of "tone" by the
> reader, one of the more common mistakes is the lack
> of formality. Yes, you want to befriend your clients—
> to a point. You want to develop a comfort level and a
> good rapport. However, it's easy to take it too far if
> you begin treating them like a long lost buddy.
> Remember that these are professionals you are
> dealing with; they must be treated with the
> appropriate level of respect and formality. Read and
> re-read e-mails before you click send to be certain
> that the tone and level of familiarity you want to
> project is correct.

Of course, expectation management does not end when the
sale is complete and the product is delivered. You, as a
sales professional, must follow the process through to its
completion and that includes the follow up after the sell.
This is where you will learn what to do and what NOT to do
the next time.

Follow up for feedback from the client can help you
understand how close you were to fulfilling their
expectations. Do not be afraid to ask for this feedback as
even negative feedback. Although potentially bruising to
your ego, it will be extremely valuable to your long-term

sales career. Again, with a sincere approach, you must ask them for their perception of your performance throughout the entire process. Was your communication with them what they had hoped? Was the delivery of the product or the performance of the service what they had expected? If not, why?

Soliciting feedback, both positive and negative, will do several things. First, it will be a clear indication to the client that you are genuinely concerned about them. Second, it will demonstrate that you are continually looking for ways to improve—a message not lost on clients who demand top performance. Third, it will set the stage for the next time you have contact with this client.

If you find that the feedback you receive is positive in every way, fantastic! But don't break your arm patting yourself on the back. That's not why you solicit feedback. With positive feedback and responses, you know you did things right. You also know that you'll want to repeat it, so you will want to store this information away for future use. Equally, if the feedback you receive is negative, you will want to store that information away as well to be certain you don't repeat those errors. It also gives you the opportunity to stand behind the level of service you promised (and the level of service they expected) by performing the damage control that's required and fixing the problem at hand.

❖ *No Excuse!* Action Item That Works #6:
   *Practice quick response time!*

> Have you ever lost a deal because something came up and you just forgot to reply to a client? Have you ever had to do relationship damage control simply because you didn't check in with a client or with your

company?  How many hours have you spent messing around with issues that could have been easily avoided by developing the habit of a quick response time?  Although the amount of email, phone, and text messages you receive in a given day might be overwhelming, and you simply feel there aren't enough hours in the day to get through them all, guess what?  TOUGH!  You knew that the sales world wasn't going to be a cakewalk, and you know that effective and timely communication is part of the deal. So, how can anyone sit back and say, "I just didn't have time?"  You must make the time to reply to inquiries, internal or external, within 24 hours. These tasks are all part of a sales process and must be incorporated into your schedule.  If you need to carve out time at the beginning or at the end of a day to accomplish this, you must get it done!  If not, you will find yourself in a continual "catch up" mode that will distract you from your goals.

When and if your delivery doesn't go as planned, you must be front and center to address the issues.  Do NOT bury your head in the sand and go missing when these problems arise.  Remember how we spoke about becoming "that guy" in the world of sales?  If you avoid following up and avoid your clients, you're well on your way down a path that you do not want to be on!   Good or bad—demonstrate to your clients that you've made a commitment to them and that you are prepared to be their partner over the long haul.

💣 Don't #3: *Don't lie to your COMPANY!*

Speaking of commitment, something that is easy for a sales professional to forget is the company that hired you to be a member of their team.   As another key component to the

*No Excuse!* mindset is that you remove the excuse of "the company." So often in sales it is easy to blame the company for your failures and woes. Why? Simply put, the company is an all-encompassing target that incorporates managers, co-workers, support staff, and everyone else that's a part of it. When a banker can't get a loan approved for a client, it's the company that was the problem. When a proposal did not get done on time, it's the company who set up the procedure that takes too long. When a delivery is not made on time, it's the company who didn't hire quality delivery people. Do you see a pattern here?

What sales people tend to forget is that they too are the "company." It's common sense that a sales person may not be able to change policies, procedures, or hiring practices. What a sales person CAN control is their OWN PERFORMANCE!

DON'T MAKE EXCUSES!

In hiring you, a company has made a commitment to you. Granted, this may not be a permanent commitment, but you knew that already. Should that affect how you approach dealing with your company? Absolutely not! You need to make a commitment to your company and stick with it.

When you wake up in the morning and head to work, you need to decide if you are 100% with the company and with the team or if you're not. If you are, terrific! This means that you've removed the "excuse" that the company is preventing you from succeeding. If you're not, it's obvious that there are poisonous issues creeping into your mindset that will not only destroy the team in which you are a part of, but it will also destroy your path to reaching the expectations you've set for yourself.

If you're not prepared to give it your all *every single day*, then you're not 100% committed, and its time to find a new sandbox to play in.   After all, you sold yourself to the company on your skills, abilities, drive, and ambition.   If things aren't going as well as you'd hoped and you're making excuses, you do nothing but an injustice to yourself and the company that's made a commitment to you.

Managing the expectations of your personal goals, your client's, or your company's isn't necessarily something that comes naturally.   Those around you that are successful in business have mastered the skills necessary to balance these expectations.  This mastery comes with time and experience.  Other times, it comes from learning from your mistakes.  This chapter is designed to provide you with suggestions on how to plan your approach before you have to make some of the common mistakes.   It was mentioned before, "The early bird gets the worm, but the second mouse gets the cheese!"   If you choose to rush headlong into your career without the proper planning—planning that incorporates the challenges to overcome before, during, and after the sale— you are doomed to make easily avoidable mistakes.  No one looks to have the mousetrap slam on their head, but everyone wants the cheese!   Prepare yourself, beginning with managing all expectations. You will find not only the cheese in the trap, but you'll find the right way to open the fridge to get at the goodies inside!

Don't forget, though, that there are a LOT of mice out there looking for the "cheddar."   You've learned so far about how to deliver to your clients and manage expectations.  Now is the time to learn about managing assets!

# CHAPTER 3: Asset Management

*"Never underestimate the power of dreams and the influence of the human spirit. We are all the same in this notion: The potential for greatness lives within each of us."*

~ Wilma Rudolph

(The first American woman runner to win three gold medals at a single Olympics)

The power of "underestimation" is a dangerous thing in the world of business and especially in the world of sales. So far you are learning about your value, your personal sense of drive and ambition, and how NOT to fall into some of the traps that bring great sales professionals to their knees. As you've been told, when you follow your passion, it's easier to understand how your personal value and your mindset affect what you do. You need to be sure that you never, EVER underestimate your own talents and your ability to be an excellent sales professional.

Too often individuals underestimate their own value, their own skill set, and their own role in the process. To date, we've discussed how to effectively deliver to your clients and your company, and we've discussed how to manage your processes. This, in turn, increases your value. Your clients will see your value through your delivery, follow up, and sincerity. Your company will see your value through your consistency and performance. Hopefully, at this point, you are understanding better how your mindset, your attitude, and the concept of *NO EXCUSE* will affect each day. This includes removing the self-deprecation that leads to negativity and the consequences that come along with it.

With success comes better self-esteem. But now it's time to talk in greater detail about the assets that can keep you on the path of success. Every sales process requires assets that must be managed effectively in order to get positive results—and we're not talking about your new smartphone that will help you keep appointments. We're talking about HUMAN assets—those around you that affect the entire sales process from co-workers to acquaintances to your competition. Yes, you must never underestimate your value within the sales process. Forget about the other assets that you must manage, and all of your positive thinking will suddenly become useless.

So, now that we've learned about the things that can affect your career related to "self," let's start working on the trap of underestimating the people related to the process that also affects your performance and your career.

**?** *No Excuse!* Question #3:
  How did you END your day today?

> ➤ Answer: This should be no different than how you started your day—with *NO EXCUSE!* Today was a perfect day to practice your craft, to hone your skills, to make an impact on your own career. So... how did it go? You started your day with the right mindset: to work hard to make today your best day. Was it? Sometimes the problem is that even with the best of plans, your day might not have ended up the way you wanted it to. Is this reason to fear tomorrow? ABSOLUTELY NOT! When it becomes time for reflection, why wasn't today your best day? What happened during the day that affected your performance?
>
> Reflect. Examine. Ask questions of yourself. When you do, you'll find out why today was or was not your best day. If it was a great day, then you

know what to do tomorrow. If it was not your best day, it's time to change something. However, you must always remember that whatever it was that made your day skew in the wrong direction, there is *NO EXCUSE!* Don't blame your boss for your bad day. Don't blame your clients for your bad day. Take accountability for what happened and make sure you do not repeat it.

When you do take accountability for the day and pledge to yourself that tomorrow is a new day and a fresh start, you're proving to yourself that your mindset of *No Excuse!* is becoming stronger. This MUST become natural to you—and in time, it will! Tomorrow is another day to practice your craft, and you should be looking forward to it, not dreading it!

When it comes to "Asset Management" as it relates to human assets, the key is to avoid underestimating those around you. Although we could discuss every human interaction that may affect your sales success, we need to bring focus to those major aspects so that you can target your energies to manage what is most likely to impact your performance.

💣 Don't #1: *Don't underestimate others!*

Sounds vague, doesn't it? "Underestimating others" seems like we might start discussing every human interaction that you would have, and that would take forever! So, let's define "others" for the purposes of this topic. Others, as it relates to your sales process, needs to include the key players within that process. For every sales process, this is quite different, and you'll have to do your due diligence to determine who will be the key players involved.

Of course, your client/prospect is key. You cannot, under any circumstances, underestimate what they bring to the process. A perfect example relayed to me recently is that of sales people in a banking environment. A friend who spent years in the financial services universe told me of the many, many times she heard the phrase, "Oh, they're probably not talking to anyone else about this loan, so this should be a slam dunk." Only then, they were blindsided when the deal was lost to another bank. Why? The sales person (in this case, the lender) underestimated their client. They made a false assumption that they wouldn't do their homework and examine all of their options. The result: The lender didn't put their best foot forward, finding out only after the sale was lost that there was another iron in the fire.

Another common example, one that you may have run into already and one which I personally have run into: Recall, if you will, the last time you held a sales meeting or presentation that included half a dozen people. As you know, sometimes these meetings are so large because the company would like to get everyone's opinion on the product or service being discussed. It seems, from first glance that there are one or two major decision makers in the room and the rest are along for the ride. So, naturally, you'll pay attention to those you THINK are the decision makers. You perfect your "schpeel" and your "pitch" with those key players in mind. But have you ever found out later that "so-and-so" sitting at the end of the table who didn't say a word was the deciding factor in going with your competition instead of with you?

How on EARTH did that happen?  It's simple: You underestimated the importance of others involved in the process.  Who is to blame?  If you've been paying attention, you know the answer:  It's you, and no one else, because you don't buy into excuses and playing the blame-game, right?  Don't worry; you're learning.  Keep going.

❖ *No Excuse!* Action Item That Works #7:
 *Be available!*

> A high value trait that many clients associate with a "partner," not just a sales person, is availability. When there is a problem or issue, the last thing you want is a valued client to have to "track you down" to get an answer.  Therefore, you need to automate yourself so that you can be available no matter when it is and no matter where you are.

> Of course, you can't be available 24/7, but that doesn't that mean that you have to *manage the expectations?*  We talked about that!  When you're not available, your clients will want to know.  But at the same time, as part of your valued service, you will be letting them know that they aren't being left out in the cold!  Have your assistant, your co-worker, or someone in the support department make sure that your client has this information when you're not available.  However, when you ARE supposed to be available, you better be certain that you can be reached.

What is the moral of this section?  Underestimating the strengths, abilities, or importance of the people around you can only lead to your downfall.  Reflect on your career to this point and answer this question honestly: "Has my underestimation of others led to me losing a deal?" If you answer honestly, you'll know the answer is yes. We've all done it—even the best sales people have done it. Maybe it was not by intent, but it was simply by omission. Either way, there was a component of your mindset that prevented you from seeing the importance of an individual within the process. Those that become better sales people remove that "excuse" for losing the sale by being better prepared. How can this be accomplished?

### 💣 Don't #2: *Don't underestimate networking!*

Networking is a great way to avoid some of these pitfalls. Most of you have probably heard the phrase, "It's not what you know, it's WHO you know." When it comes to sales, preparation is extremely important and that includes understanding the people that are involved in the process. As such, building your network can be an excellent way to help boost your performance simply by connecting with more people!

Social networking in today's sales environment can be extremely beneficial. Of course, it's imperative that you keep your business and personal social networking SEPARATE. We've all seen or heard of countless situations where a personal social networking comment has come back to bite someone. As you develop your professional relationships and your network, it's more and more likely that your profiles will be reviewed by your prospects, clients, and even your competition that are looking to find something to use against you.

Effective management of your social networks will be important. There are plenty of options out there, but when it comes to professionals, the go-to social media site is

LinkedIn. This, for the most part, is the site for those that want to develop professional networks and not for those who want to tell us what they had for lunch or that they just got a bad sunburn. Make developing your network part of your daily/weekly routine. By requesting connections on social networking sites, you increase your chances of having a connection with that elusive prospect which just might be your "in."

❖ *No Excuse!* Action Item That Works #8:
   *Protect your reputation with appearances!*

Everyone has heard the term "keeping up appearances," but this has a negative connotation, doesn't it? It gives you the impression that something is fake, artificial, or simply for the benefit of the crowd.

When we say that "appearances" are a key *No Excuse!* Action Item, we mean it in the most positive sense. Personal appearances at company or other corporate functions demonstrate a dedication and commitment that everyone is looking for in a sales partner and/or employee. The real key, however, is to be sure that whatever appearance this may be, that it is sincere. Those that go to an event "because they have to" stand out like a zebra among penguins. All too often I've heard co-workers state, "I'm just going to go so that the president can see that I showed up." That "showing up" is painfully transparent and goes directly back to "don't underestimate others." When you attend an event, it MUST be clear that you are there at your own freewill. Don't sit like a lump in a corner pouting. Make it your chance to build your connections and demonstrate that you really care! If you don't, then don't go! It does more harm to your reputation than you may think!

Of course, face-to-face networking is the best way to go. In that way, you can make that personal connection and have an opportunity to strike up an actual conversation (what a concept!). Begin researching professional organizations within your industry. Typically major groups have monthly or quarterly meetings where members get together to discuss topics of interest, or possibly just to meet for a drink after work. Either way, if you aren't in front of them, they will never know you exist. Does your company take part in any Chamber meetings or "Business After Hours" events? If so, be sure to get involved and take part. Want to make a real impact? Start a "Business After Hours" event yourself, and get your company to sponsor it!

✖ *No Excuse!* Salesology Principle #3:
*Birds of a feather flock together, but Eagles fly above the rest!*

We just mentioned starting your own "Business After Hours" event. This is a perfect example of setting yourself apart from the "flock." Successful sales people know, and this book imparts to you, that it's all about the effort you put in versus the effort of your competition. The *value* that you bring to your company and your clients is what leads to your success. It's about making "one more call" before you go home versus what the sales person across the hall did.

When you take those extra steps to add value to the business relationships that you're going to spend a lot of time building, you WILL reap the rewards. It's one thing to be a bird in the flock, going in the same direction, doing the same thing. When was the last time you heard anyone mention that "majestic soaring *pigeon?*" Be the stand out that you want to be—the stand out that you KNOW you can be. Just take the extra steps that your competition does not— and stop "flocking" around!

By developing your networks, both online and in person, you will find that making that key connection which could make or break a deal will be much easier. Additionally, you'll find that your successes can be more easily relayed to both your clients and your competitors. Did you just wrap up a deal with a big name in the industry? One that would make your clients stand up and say, "Wow! If he can help them, he CERTAINLY can help me!" How will you get that information in front of those that matter? NETWORKING! Keep this top-of-mind as you develop your career, since the connection made today may make all the difference tomorrow.

Now, I mentioned that networking is a great way to let your competition know that you or your company has accomplished something. Make no mistake: Your competition is looking for a similar advantage!

### ♦ Don't #3: *Don't underestimate your competition!*

You've seen it before: a newspaper or magazine article about your competitor highlighting that new person brought on board. Or, what about the online posting about the new business relationship developed that demonstrates your competitor's ability to deal with the big players in the industry? In a more common example, your bid lost out to someone else because they were able to do the job for 10% less money than you.

If your company is the last to innovate, it will be the first to fail. This holds true in your own personal approach to sales and business development. Although you personally may not have the chance to change the direction of your company, you DO have the chance to change your methods to react to the changes in the environment around you. What do I mean? Well, if your company is no longer an innovator and your competition knows it, you may be at a disadvantage. Don't think for a minute that your competitor isn't bringing that up to your prospect, so you best be prepared with a new approach that highlights what makes you better, because they're doing the same thing!

Sun Tzu, in his classic text *The Art of War* stated, "He who exercises no forethought but makes light of his opponents is sure to be captured by them." There is no more poignant phrase than this to describe how underestimating your competition, your *opponent,* will lead to disaster.

Let's use a real-world example: Blockbuster. The 500-pound gorilla in the movie rental universe for years filed for bankruptcy and closed store after store. Why? Because they *underestimated their competition.* As Netflix, iTunes, and Redbox came into being, Blockbuster continued down their own path, failing to understand that they weren't just a provider of movie and game rentals; they were a distributor of entertainment. By concentrating on brick-and-mortar locations throughout the country and convincing themselves that this was the only way to go, other distributors developed a new plan: online rentals, automated kiosks, and through-the-mail rentals. Their competition developed a way to "distribute entertainment" at a much lower cost, forcing the 500-pound gorilla to go on a crash diet. When all was said and done, their efforts were too little, too late, and they've become a textbook example of how underestimating the competition leads to colossal failure.

Are you doing this? Are you overlooking the abilities of your competitors? Remember, no matter how successful you or your company are today, tomorrow brings no guarantees. You need to pay attention to the trends and advances that can threaten your sales existence in order to adjust your method and style.

❖ *No Excuse!* Action Item That Works #9:
   *Know when to walk away!*

> There are times in a sales person's career that you just can't land the sale no matter what you do. No...really! It happens! Remember, just because you receive a "no" today doesn't mean you'll receive a "no" tomorrow, so make sure you're setting yourself up for that success down the road by understanding when to simply walk away. Your sales reputation is at stake with every meeting you hold and every hand you shake. Appearing desperate during a sales process can lead you down the path of failure in several ways: 1) your prospect may wonder why you're so desperate for the sale; 2) you may say things that will prevent a prospect from calling you the next time; or 3) you may be putting your company at risk.
>
> I personally have heard sales people say, "Well, if they can do it for X, I'll do it for X minus 5%." What does that really say to a prospect? One, it says you're lazy and don't want to sharpen the pencil;

you'll just wait for a bid and undercut them. Two, it says you don't really care about their needs; you're just ready to take the easy way out. Three, it demonstrates that you haven't sold the value of the product or service, and you're just making it all about price.

If you're beat, you're beat. There's nothing wrong with acknowledging that as long as you have a valid reason for it. If your company simply can't offer the same price, so be it. Next time, sell the VALUE instead of the price. If you can't meet a deadline and your competition can, so be it. Next time, address the timing issue up front. In short, understand why you didn't make the sale, acknowledge your deficiency, and promise that next time you'll work twice as hard to make it work. Then, walk away with your reputation intact and get ready for the next meeting.

Remember the *No Excuse!* Salesology Principle in this chapter: Eagles fly above the rest. It's about going the extra distance to stand above the rest. It means, simply, that you must be putting in the effort to be the best you can be, and if you don't, the people around you will take advantage of your lack of effort and pass you by.

When you underestimate those around you, the value of building a strong network, and your competition, you inevitably will be met with the results of that underestimation. You will see people around you getting ahead while you seem to be stuck in neutral. You will see your high value prospects continually signing with your competition because you've missed something. Note what was said: because "YOU" have missed something. Avoid the blame game pitfalls. "My company hasn't come out with a new product for years." "I didn't get the chance to place a bid because that person never contacted us." "How was I supposed to know that?" All of these are excuses made by someone not going above and beyond to learn, study, and develop themselves into a winner.

It's the lazy sales person's way out to blame others. If you take nothing else from what you're reading, make sure you take away that your success or failure is dependent SOLEY upon your effort, drive, and ambition. The chapters you've read to this point are designed to continually drive into your psyche that *No Excuse!* Selling is a mindset that cannot waiver if you wish to be successful!

We've spoken here, briefly, about developing contacts and building your network in order to reap the benefits down the road. The question is this: How do you best go about harvesting the fruits of your labor?

# CHAPTER 4: Leveraging Relationships

*"People have been known to achieve more as a result of working with others than against them."* ~ Dr. Allan Fromme

Using the term "leveraging" can mean, to some, "taking advantage." Guess what? That's true! But it's not something that should be viewed as negative simply because you are utilizing the tools at your disposal. In most situations, when you are developing a business relationship, it is to leverage the alliance you've created down the road. Often, these relationships result in win-win situations for everyone involved; other times, it is to give you an advantage in a situation over an opponent or competitor. Remember, in developing a business relationship they (your contact) have received something of value from you in the past, and they likely have the expectation of returning that value in some form in the future.

These individuals already know you, and they have an opinion of you. You've worked hard (hopefully) to keep these relationships strong and active. So, when the time is right, you need to be sure you're leveraging these relationships.

Here is a great example: On *The Apprentice*, Donald Trump's television show where celebrities are brought in to compete against one another, a challenge was put forth to the two groups: selling cupcakes. It was fairly simple: Whoever made the most money won the challenge. One group put together a marketing plan and tried to sell a lot of cupcakes on a New York street corner. The other group set out to pick up the phone and call their friends, asking, "Would you be willing to buy a dozen cupcakes for $5,000?

The money will go to charity." The friends said sure, and of course, they won the challenge.

Was this cheating? Absolutely NOT! One team simply used their relationships in a very creative, intelligent way. Did they "take advantage" of their friends? Of course not, because their friends could have said no just as easily as they said yes.

? *No Excuse!* Question #4:
  *How much time did you spend networking yourself today?*

> ➤ The right answer is NOT ENOUGH! No matter how much time you spent today building your network or reaching out to your existing relationships to strengthen the ties, it's never enough! Are you gathering how important this component of sales is? Don't make building your network a "once-in-a-while" thing. You need to be vigilant daily by reaching out to those you don't know and reaching out to those you DO know to ask for a new name, a new lead, and a new connection.

In order to effectively leverage your working relationships, there are a few things you need to be sure you do, and things to be sure you do NOT do so that you can keep a good balance. We will discuss these points in detail throughout this chapter. This includes making sure that your contacts know who you are looking to meet, reciprocating their efforts, and keeping yourself top-of-mind.

But let's start with a common problem and an easy trap to fall into: over-dependence on your network, references, or contacts.

### ◆⋇ Don't #1: *Don't abuse your referrals!*

True, contact and referrals are available to utilize when the time is right. However, you'll want to avoid turning a referral into a crutch for yourself. This holds true for references used in the more common job interview scene or for references to receive an introduction. First, no matter how long it's been since you've spoken with a reference and no matter how many times you have used this person as a reference, always check with them before using their name!

Let's use a common example, which happened to a close acquaintance of mine. His name is John, and he went to an interview for a new position at another company. After a great interview, John wound up not getting that job. He later found out that his interviewer knew his current manager as the interviewer worked for him in the past. Unfortunately, John neglected to discuss this with his current manager who would have instructed him NOT to use his name as a reference. Instead, not only did he miss out on a job opportunity, he lost credibility with his current manager. In no uncertain terms, this was a total backfire!

You need to be certain, as part of your continuous relationship building methodology, that you not only keep your references and contacts up to date, but you need to make sure they stay well informed! The intent of using a reference is to be sure that the results are positive. Your contacts and connections can't read your mind, so you need to brief them on what your goals are and alert them to any upcoming communications they may expect! The last thing you want is for a contact to receive a call and answer with, "Wow, I haven't talked with him in over a year! What's he up to these days?"

*No Excuse!* Salesology Principle #4:
*If you think you CAN or think you CAN'T, you're right.*

> Although somewhat cliché and something you may have heard before, this simple phrase can have a profound effect on your day, your year, or your career. *No Excuse*! Selling is, say it with me, a *mindset*. You must remove the negativity that can keep you beaten down and miserable. A simple way to do that is to remind yourself that you CAN accomplish the goals that you've set for yourself. Will accomplishing your goals be easy? Probably not. But if you're looking for a self-fulfilling prophecy, continue to tell yourself that there's no way you can do it—because you'll be right. When you spiral into a mindset of defeat, that's what will occur. Turn that around and get yourself in the mindset of "can do!"

Of course, there's the flip side: using references and contacts too much. The people you've built business relationships with are busy people, just like you. They have their own issues, goals, challenges, and other things that take up time each day. Quite honestly, although good references and contacts are usually willing to help, they can quickly turn into a liability if you're hounding them or taking up their valuable time.

You have to be cautious in this regard. Utilize references when you know there's a connection with someone, not just a blind referral. Make sure you're as well informed about a situation as you can be, so it can be relayed well to your reference. No one likes to be blind-sided, so help them to help you! Finally, make sure you use these references and relationships sparingly in a structured pattern to assure that they'll be there for you when you *really* need it.

## ☀ Don't #2: *Don't be afraid to ask!*

An odd "don't" to be sure, but over the years, I've heard this time and again: "They never asked." From asking your long-term crush out on that first date to asking the CEO of a multi-billion dollar organization for their business, you HAVE TO ASK! I can personally relay dozens of example where I was told I won the business because I asked for it. I've trained sales executives who knew how to develop a well flowing presentation and answer every objection, but when it came down to it, they never asked, "Did we earn your business today?"

Again, you work hard to develop relationships for the long term in order to leverage them down the road when the time is right. You have to learn to be comfortable with the "ask." Start with recommendations from your relationships, which cost nothing! When you know you've done a great job and gone that extra mile, take a moment to confirm that everything is ok with your client, and then ask for a recommendation. A simple letter or e-mail written to "someone in the future" can speak volumes. It can also mean the difference between earning new business versus losing out on an opportunity because you didn't demonstrate your past accomplishments.

You must also be sure to ask for referrals from your existing contact base as well. Of course, referring back to what we talked about earlier, not abusing your references, you'll want to make sure that your timing is right. But at the end of the day, you need to ask your existing relationships for referrals, and if you've done a good job for them they should be happy to provide you with a name or two that could benefit from what you're offering!

Too often I've heard under-performing sales people make the EXCUSE of "I don't have any new leads coming in!" My response: That's garbage! That person is the poster-child for laziness, and it's someone you do NOT want to model yourself after. These people are the "shooting stars," and you don't want to be a shooting star. Shooting stars shine brightly, create gasps and a moment of wonder, but burn out fast and are never seen again. These are the cherry pickers that aren't quite sure how to develop new business; they can only close what's right in front of them.

❖ *No Excuse!* Action Item That Works #10:
   *Create perceived value!*

> Have you ever noticed that there's always a "go-to" guy within a company who is the best at fixing a certain problem, always seems to have the answer, or always knows who you should turn to? Now, have you noticed that many of these people are either not in a position of authority or what they're experts at isn't really part of their job description? How do you think that happens?

> Through design or by pure luck, these people have increased their perceived value within the company— and you should too! Start working yourself into a position of "perceived" authority, even if the actual authoritative role isn't available. You've probably already been there; you've heard others say (or caught yourself saying), "The boss really doesn't

know what goes on in the trenches. Ask so-and-so. They'll have the right answer." Get yourself into the role of "so-and-so." In time, your perceived value to the company will rise and THAT will give rise to new and better opportunities!

You, on the other hand, want to be that bright star that's always shining. You want to be the constant light in the sky that's strong and consistent. You do this by finding ways to develop new business on your own, by leveraging the relationships you've developed, asking for referrals, and creating a long-term approach to your career. It's imperative that you learn this skill early as every month that passes, where you've not expanded your network, your contacts are nothing more than lost opportunities that are impossible to measure.

And when it comes down to the opportunities themselves, if you don't ask, you won't receive! You have worked very hard to develop a level of comfort, trust, and sincerity between you and your clients, so why would it be difficult to ask for their business? You've demonstrated a sincere desire to help them by providing top-notch service and support. The time will come where they will have an opportunity to repay you for your hard work with additional business, but you cannot forget to ask for it!

Remember, and I can't stress it enough, you've worked to develop key relationships with many different people at every level, but you eventually will need to leverage those relationships for your benefit! If you do not, you will find a great deal of hard work going to waste. Of course, once you DO ask, you definitely can't forget to give something back!

💣 Don't #3: *Don't forget to give back!*

You will likely develop relationships that, today, may not be able to help you with referrals or information. Don't forget that this relationship will also be looking to you to help THEM on occasion as well. Any relationship development needs to be done with a long-term approach so be certain to treat it as such. Much like a garden that may take years to cultivate, water, feed, and prune before reaching its full potential, so are your business relationships.

Certainly you don't need to wait until you receive help or benefit in order to provide help or benefit. Think about your top 10 clients right now. When was the last time you sent any new referrals or business their way? How far do you think a new name or contact sent their way might go with your chances of earning their business the next time it comes up? You certainly don't want to send junk their way, which would lead to a perception of "this person is wasting my time sending me these people," but each reference doesn't need to be a slam-dunk new piece of business for them either.

It's the effort here that counts. Sending to your contacts a quality lead here and there goes a long, long way to proving not only that you're paying attention, but that you are genuinely concerned about their company as well. If they know that, why wouldn't they offer you their next piece of business?

Another way to give back and add value is by simply keeping in contact with your relationships. Think back to the last lead that was sent to you by someone in your contact pool. How did it turn out? Did you ever get through to the person? Was there an opportunity to discuss or wasn't there? Now, did you let the person who gave you that lead know how things went? Keep in mind that your contacts want to know how things are going and if leads/referrals do or don't work out. Again, if they don't, that's ok. It gives you an opportunity to tell them how much you appreciate the effort, so don't miss out on that change. Whether it went well or if it went poorly, those that referred it to you want to know, so be sure your lines of communication are always open!

❖ *No Excuse!* Action Item That Works #11: *Communicate!*

> If you are finding yourself saying, "Geez, I hate picking up the phone," sales might not be for you. It seems ridiculous that there are people in sales positions that have reluctance to picking up the phone, but they're out there! Why is that? It certainly could be a degree of experience. These people may prefer face-to-face rather than over-the-phone. It is true that phone communications and in-person communications are different animals. But to be an effective sales person, striving for long-term achievements, you must overcome this reluctance quickly, or it will doom your results down the road.

> Therefore, you must develop CONFIDENCE. Invest the time and effort in yourself and learn to expect success every time you pick up the phone. Learn the skills and practice the techniques, and your confidence will grow with every call. You got into sales for a reason—for the challenge, for the thrill, whatever that may be. Do NOT let a fear of picking up the phone keep you from the goals you've set for yourself! Do not be afraid to make a mistake, as it's your chance to learn. To quote Henry Ford, "Failure

is only the opportunity to begin again more intelligently."

One more simple, yet incredibly effective way to give back to those in your business relationship pool is to tell them "Thanks!" Everyone likes to be acknowledged, so be sure to send out a quick note on random occasions, not just the standard holidays. Buy a 50-pack of blank thank-you cards and send them to 50 people. Send out a quick e-mail, or better yet leave a quick voicemail to let them know you appreciate their past business and that you're looking forward to helping them in the future.

But don't go overboard! A small token gift is one thing, but make sure you keep it professional and sincere. A gift card to download some music, a googly-eyed fuzz ball to stick on their computer, or even a smiley face on a post it note—anything that will show that you truly appreciate the relationship you've developed will go a long way and will take very little effort.

❖ *No Excuse!* Action Item That Works #12:
   *Be firm!*

The words "bargaining" and "haggling"—ever thought about the difference between them? It's a fine line between the two, but knowing which you're doing can really make the difference in finalizing a sale or having the door hit you on the way out. Haggling with someone—over the terms of a major deal or over which movie to go see at the theater—simply means that you're in an argumentative state. Usually haggling is based on emotion, which means you haven't effectively sold the perceived value of whatever it is you're trying to sell!

Bargaining, on the other hand, is a good thing! This means that you're actually close to a deal, and you're working to fine tune minor points. It should tell you that your client or prospect has understood the core of what you are selling but has a differing opinion on some of the details. This is when logical, composed discussions take place—not the hodge-podge of emotional outbursts that happen when you're haggling with someone.

Be sure to pay attention! If you can define what you're doing with a prospect as haggling, then it's time to pause and take stock of the situation. If you find that you're bargaining with each other over some details, then you're close to notching another win!

As stated at the beginning, many believe that "leveraging" and "taking advantage of" are one in the same. This is, of course, not the case, but you certainly can start to be viewed in the latter if you abuse your relationships and if you don't properly reciprocate. Networking and relationship management are both huge weapons in the arsenal of the successful sales person, but many of these "common sense" points aren't as common sense as you might think—especially when you become busy and bogged down in your day-to-day sales functions.

Every day you are working, or you SHOULD be working, to develop new relationships and strengthen existing relationships. Be sure to pay attention to the nuances of this component of sales, as they are just as important to the end result as an effective presentation. Also be sure to utilize these relationships when the time is right, which should wind up being beneficial to everyone involved.

This leads us into our final chapter. How does all of this intertwine? How does your performance, your communication, and your business relationships weave itself into a successful sales career? It starts by guiding you through the differences between "Selling" and "Sales."

# CHAPTER 5: Sell vs. Sales

*"Successful people ask better questions, and as a result, they get better answers."*
~ Tony Robbins

What a cryptic thing to say..."Sell vs. Sales." What does that mean? In short, it means there is a HUGE difference between "sales" and the function, the job, the career of "selling." Sales are what are on the report at the end of the month, on the tote board in the sales team's offices, and on the commission check you earn. "Selling" is what you do every day, and it's why you got into selling in the first place. It's also the reason why you've read this book, because you want to improve yourself so that you can sell better, which *in turn* leads to more sales.

Sales is a career path that you've chosen for your own unique reason. Whatever that reason may be, there is no possible way that you've seen all that there is to see and experienced all that there is to experience. The goal of this chapter is to highlight some additional points about what makes one sales person a rousing success and why another washes out after their first year. This begins with understanding that you are always "selling." You're selling yourself to your co-workers, your new clients, your long-term clients, and your prospects. If you are not doing your job in this aspect, the "sales" won't be there.

The trick is to not wonder why you're washing out but to avoid getting to that point in the first place. As we have said time and again throughout this book, it's all about *No Excuse!* When you remove the obstacles that you believe are standing in your way, real or perceived, you can begin focusing your limited time and energy on the task at hand: building your sales.

❖ *No Excuse!* Action Item That Works #13:
*Understand personality!*

It's no secret that everyone is different. Each person you deal with throughout the day has a different drive, a different set of goals, and a different way of doing things. One of the challenges for Type-A, aggressive sales people is conforming to the personality of the client. Most people are so set in their ways that it winds up getting in the way of sales success.

Understanding the preferences of your clients or prospects makes a huge difference, and it all comes down to their personality. For example, an associate of mine was born and raised in the Midwest. As such, he's a bit of a storyteller. He prefers to educate, train, and sell with a "storyteller" approach much like watching a movie, set the stage, make sure everyone understands the goal, tell the story, and get the end result. This is a fantastic approach as long as the client shares the same personality. Now, when he needs to deal with someone from the East Coast, he is forced to change his style and approach. He must adapt to a "just get to the point" mentality, bullet-point his thoughts, and make quick presentations. Is he comfortable doing this? Not so much, but he also knows that if he doesn't adapt to the preference of the prospect, he's sunk.

Once you've removed the obstacles, you can begin to think clearly about what changes or new skills you need to make in order to move in the right direction and to avoid the pitfalls of those around you that are washing out!

### ● Don't #1: *Don't let "sales" determine a relationship!*

A common mistake made by those that are classic "shooting star" sales people is that the value of a client, prospect, or overall relationship is based on past sales. These people pay attention ONLY to those who have brought them sales (and therefore, income) in the past, while virtually ignoring everyone else. We talked previously about avoiding turning into "that guy." A gigantic pet peeve with a buyer is that their sales person disappears when there isn't any new business to offer. In somewhat exaggerated terms, this type of sales person will contact a client to see if there is any new business in the works, and if there isn't, the reply is, "Ok, I'll call you again next year to see how things are going."

What kind of message does this send to the prospect? More importantly, what kind of message do you think they're sharing about this particular pathetic sales person? It definitely doesn't show that there is a genuine interest in their company, and it most certainly doesn't project any level of sincerity! What it does show is that the prospects value has a direct correlation to the amount of sales that has been provided, much like a dog that doesn't make a mess on the carpet only because there are treats involved.

Although it again sounds like common sense, staying in touch with your contacts whether there is any business is to your benefit! The common sense reasons of staying in front of them on a regular basis keep your business presence fresh. You don't have a crystal ball to tell you when they'll have a business opportunity for you, so you must make it an ingrained habit to continually keep in touch with these relationships. You just never know when that next big offer might be on the way. Also, because you lack a crystal ball, you just never know when a small account might suddenly become a top 10! Don't be caught off guard because you didn't put in the effort.

This goes hand-in-hand with the effort you're putting in. You must be certain you are spending the same amount of time and putting in the same level of dedication to the smaller accounts as you do your top 10. This may be counter-intuitive: spending as much time on small accounts as you do on larger accounts. However, we're talking about relationship here and those small clients know people who know people. Ignore the wrong client one too many times, and word can spread among a business community like wildfire. Now, instead of spending quality time and effort building and developing relationships, you're relegated to damage control while you attempt to explain why Customer X just isn't as important as Customer Y. To quote someone you may have heard of, Mr. Sam Walton, "There is only one boss: the customer, and he can fire everybody in the company from the chairman on down, simply by spending his money somewhere else." There is no question that this is a rock-solid truth. Never forget it.

❖ *No Excuse!* Action Item That Works #14:
   *Send positive press!*

> There is no shortage of gloom and doom in the business world today. There will always be some sort of negative press to be found. But, does this make

your clients and prospects want to move forward with their decisions to purchase from you?

Take time now and again to find a positive spin on the industries of your clients to infuse a bit of uplifting news.  And don't think that's an impossible task; it simply takes a little effort.  Highlighting an effort by a local bank that is helping people purchase homes may be great news to someone working in the lumber industry.  Recent news about security breaches at companies who wind up losing data could be good news to that IT company you're working with to help them land some new business.  Gas prices that are getting people down may be welcome news to a dealership selling motorcycles.

A little effort looking for the positives in today's press as it relates to your clients might go a long way toward you landing an unexpected piece of business, so stay alert and stay positive!

Speaking of effort, as we talked about before, everyone wants to be recognized and appreciated.  Your client that bought 1 widget from you 6 months ago deserves to be appreciated for buying that widget from YOU instead of your competition.  No matter where someone falls on the "sales volume" list, it's always going to be to your benefit to thank them for choosing you and to let them know you're looking forward to the next time you can help them with their business needs.  What does this let them know?  This lets them know that you're not just "selling" for today.

💣* Don't #2: *Don't just sell for today!*

Any successful sales executive knows that what you do, or don't do, today affects what happens tomorrow, next month, or next year. You must always be aware that your inaction is as important as your action. When the iron cools, you cannot become complacent because you never know when business is going to heat up. When it does, you are either going to be prepared to capitalize on the opportunity or you will let it pass you by. By planning ahead you will be ready for the opportunities that will come your way.

Here is a story that sums up this concept:

When I worked at an auto dealership, I knew two car salesmen: Bill and James. Bill was a fast runner and always beat everyone out to the car lot to meet the prospects. James got tired of Bill beating him to the car lot, so he decided to stay inside and make prospect calls. The car lot manager always laughed because his entire sales staff would run out to the lot when a new customer would show up—at least everyone, except James.

After 3 years, the manager noticed Bill was still running out to the lot, but James never did. The manager checked James' car sales chart and found it to be better than most. So, the baffled manager went to James and asked him what his secret was. James told him it was simple: He didn't like to run, so he researched the car owner market and determined that the average U.S. citizen drives their car for 2 to 3 years. He thought ahead and built a nice book of repeat client business and referrals.

Today, he only sells to existing customers versus competing with Bill who is still the fastest runner on the lot. The moral of this story is that Bill was selling for "today" only to those right in front of him, while James figured out how to sell for tomorrow—and he saves a bundle on running shoes.

*No Excuse!* Salesology Principle #5:
*Make selling win/win!*

> Although it's true that nearly every sales function that exists is "adversarial," it certainly doesn't mean that one side must lose. Think about it: You have something to sell to someone who wants to buy. There is what you want to sell it for, and there is what the client is willing to pay. The win/win is somewhere in the middle. Your client receives the benefits and the value of the product or service you're offering, and you receive another new client and a new sale. It's all about the wins!
>
> When you approach sales as if the only "win" should be yours, that attitude will be readily transparent. Your clients will know that something's not right and that you may be trying to pull a fast one. But, when you are sincere and can demonstrate that you are looking for that win/win situation, you will find yourself more relaxed, more open, and more approachable. Every sale can be a win/win situation if you approach every sale with that mindset.

Of course, there is another moral to this story. All too often, a successful sales person will rest on their laurels. When a sale is made, celebrate! You did a great job. You had success! You get to see your name on the top of the leaderboard! But who would you rather be: the guy in first place one month in a row and then last place the next, or the one that is consistently at the top of that leaderboard?

I suppose that all depends on what motivates you. Do you enjoy the attention so much that you'll break your neck, work until 10 p.m. every night, and have one great month so that you get recognized? As long as that's part of your long-term goals, to get attention, then maybe that's fine. I would guess that your goals are more worthwhile than getting a pat on the back, though, aren't they?

Continuous effort over the long haul: THAT'S how to become a top sales person, not with the "shooting star" approach. When you're developing your business and your contacts, you're doing it not for today, but for tomorrow and next week and even next year. This is precisely why we've been discussing the importance of follow up, communication, understanding, and sincerity. Forget the clown who keeps reminding you, "I was the top sales person 2 years ago!" Good for them. But isn't that the mantra in pretty much every line of business, "What have you done for me lately?" It sure is, so make sure you're working things for the long term, and when the time is right, those sales will roll in. When they do, hopefully you hit the top of the leaderboard. Always remember though, everything starts over the next month and you better be ready! I've heard it said, "One day penthouse, next day dog house." Don't get too comfortable with today. Keep your edge. Keep moving up—steady and directly.

We've discussed the importance of effective delivery, not overpromising what you can accomplish, avoiding the trap of underestimating those around you, and even how to build and maintain your hard earned business relationships. All of these components are part of selling for tomorrow. All of this sets the stage for your next encounter with your clients and set you up well for success. But there is one final thing—an overall view of *No Excuse!* Selling that you must not forget...

### 💣 Don't #3: *Don't be mistaken!*

Make no mistake, everyone sells, but not everyone is a sales person. Let's dive into this concept a bit more because, by reading this book, you're saying, "I'm a sales person." However, if you find yourself struggling, lagging behind the rest, and not living up to your own expectations, the time might be right to decide if you are simply selling or you're a sales person.

Regarding the comment that "everyone sells," this is true, but it may not be selling in the conventional sense. During an interview, a person is selling themselves to potential employers when they highlight their skills and abilities over the competition, and then, they are selling the potential employer on their "value" when it's time to talk salary. When you walk into your manager's office to talk about a raise, you certainly have your "presentation" ready, don't you? What about the last time that you and your significant other were going to the movies and you needed to sell them on one versus the other? Selling even occurs at the dinner table when you're teaching the importance of proper table manners to your kids!

Now, you may sit back and say, "Yeah, I do all these things well." But does this mean you're a sales person at heart? Does it mean this is your PASSION? Let's use a real-world example where the odds are you know someone who's done this: selling Mary Kay or Avon cosmetics. A quote that I found that was attributed to an anonymous cosmetic sales woman states, "Most people in most businesses fail because of numerous reasons. Mainly, they don't work hard enough.

Selling isn't for just anyone, and most people realize that they don't have what it takes and only a few succeed. But if a few can succeed, doesn't that mean anyone can?"

By this logic, because Bill Gates made billions upon billions of dollars that means anyone can. Since someone swam across the English Channel, that means anyone can. WRONG! Just as, in the above quote, "Most people in most business fail because of numerous reasons," this also means that people SUCCEED for numerous reasons. When it comes to sales, having an ability to sell (as everyone does in one way, shape, or form) does not mean that everyone can succeed.

❖ *No Excuse!* Action Item That Works #15:
   Always be prospecting!

> When you inevitably find yourself in a sales downswing, you need to find out why and fix it. That's common sense of course, but are you looking at the right things? Effective, efficient prospecting is an important factor in the long-term success of any sales person. Remember we talked about not being a "shooting star?" Those are often the people who start in a new position, cherry pick the easy sales, blast through the existing list of prospects (or the prospects left behind by whoever they replaced) and have great success... in the short term.

> What they've done is fall into the misconception that sales and new prospects will always be there. Of course you need to spend the majority of your time talking with existing customers and wrapping up deals. If not, you'll never finish anything! Make that 60% of your day. Take 30% of your time to make

sure you're prospecting, speaking with new people, creating that network. Only then can you assure yourself of a constant flow of business throughout the year. What's the last 10%? Your PLAN! You can find yourself wasting a lot of your valuable, limited time if you don't spend some time planning your attack. When will you make these calls? What do you want to get accomplished by the end of the week, month, or quarter? Make sure you continuously pay attention to these components if you want to have long-term sales success!

Drive, ambition, and passion, along with talent, make a successful sales person. Those that make *NO EXCUSE* will rise above the rest! A sales person is someone who sells as a calling. It's the path they've chosen; it's the life they've chosen. As such, the most successful sales people are continually growing, learning, expanding their knowledge, and, of course, not making excuses for themselves when things go wrong. You have to put in the work! Remember the great Vince Lombardi, "The only place success comes before work is in the dictionary."

But, make sure you don't make this mistake either: a "sales person" fits a personality type. Yes, typically sales people are Type-A personalities; they are aggressive, outgoing, self-confident, etc. If that's not you, should you give up right now? Absolutely NOT! These Type-A's are often the one's that you "hear," but what about the shy, quiet personalities? They most certainly have their place in the sales universe, and they are many times preferred over the over-aggressive sales teams. These people weren't natural born sales people, but they studied, practiced, and eventually developed a method that works for them. These are the methodical, purposeful, well-organized sales people that manage to succeed, while those around them are running around! Both methods can work—if you make it work. Just as every client has a different personality, so does the average sales person. No matter which bucket you fit into best, always remember that hard work and focused effort can get you to the goals you want to reach!

**?** *No Excuse!* Question #5:
   *What did you take away from this book?*

> ➤ Here's the answer: THERE IS *NO EXCUSE!*

Here's what it boils down to: You've taken it upon yourself to enter the world of sales and the odds are good that you want to be successful at what you do. The question is this: Are you willing to remove the excuses that you're making for yourself to justify poor performance and accept that you, and ONLY you, are the one responsible?

The effort you put into it regarding training, development, organization, mentoring, and whatever that may be will mean nothing if you do not first remove the self-created roadblocks that stand in your way and cloud your vision. The excuses that are created to justify anything are the lazy salesperson's way out. Once you can look yourself in the mirror and tell yourself "I will no longer make excuses," you will be on your way. Then comes the effort, the hard work, and, eventually, the rewards.

# _Conclusion_

_"The difference between a successful person and others is not a lack of strength, not a lack of knowledge, but rather a lack of will."_
~ Vince Lombardi

Now that you've made your way through this book, what hit home for you?  Did you learn about (or maybe remember some things you've forgotten) what could be holding you back from becoming the superior sales person that you know you can be?

I will say this: By reading this book, you've taken an excellent step, so give yourself the credit you deserve! Seeing fault in one's self is not always an easy thing to do. Recognizing faults and making the commitment to improve is challenging.  Not everyone does it; not everyone WANTS to do it.  Look around you at the sales people you admire, the sales people you want to be, and also at the sales people who look miserable.  What got them to each of those separate destinations?  Surely those that are miserable in their sales job didn't start out saying, "I look forward to bringing up the rear at our company." They started out with the same drive and desire to succeed that you have.  The problem is that they lost their way.

There is always room to grow and develop.  There are always new things to learn.  With this book, you've learned that the "No Excuse!" method of sales development is step one.  Without it, everything you do or do not do will eventually land squarely back on your shoulders, and you will still be left to wonder why things aren't going your way.

Hopefully, just by reading this short book you've learned something new—about the world of sales and about yourself. Reflect on what you have read and ask yourself, "What did I take away from this?"

Now, you should have no excuses. So, until we talk again, remember that tomorrow will be your best day when you have *No Excuse!*

# *NO EXCUSE! SELLING ANTHOLOGY*

**Chapter 1 Delivery Question #1:**   What do you really want...Clients or Customers?

**Answer:**   You always want clients! What is the difference? Its simple: Customers buy from you. Clients buy into you!

**Action Item That Works #1:**   Personal Follow up works!

**Don't #1:** Don't "oversell" and "under deliver."

**Action Item That Works #2:**   Follow a routine!

**Don't #2:** Don't be caught off guard!

**Action Item That Works #3:**   Remain consistent!

**Don't #3:** Don't be "that" guy

**Salesology Principle #1:** If you do well, or you do badly, you're going to reap what you sow. Take personal responsibility, and hold yourself to a higher standard.

**Chapter 2 Expectation Management Question #2:** How did you start your day today?

**Answer:** The answer you should be saying out loud is this: "I started my day with No Excuse!"

**Action Item That Works #4:** Be sincere!

**Don't #1:** Don't lie to yourself

**Action Item That Works #5:** Understand email etiquette!

**Don't #2:** Don't lie to your Clients!

**Action Item That Works #6:** Practice quick response time!

**Don't #3:** Don't lie to your COMPANY!

**Salesology Principle #2:** The early bird gets the worm, but it's the second mouse that gets the cheese!

**Chapter 3 Asset Management Question #3:** How did you end your day today?

**Answer:** With No Excuse!

**Action Item That Works #7:** Be available!

**Don't #1:** Don't underestimate others!

**Action Item That Works #8:** Protect your reputation with appearances! Be there.

**Don't #2:** Don't underestimate networking!

**Action Item That Works #9:** Know when to walk away!

**Don't #3**: Don't underestimate your competition!

**Salesology Principle #3:** Birds of a feather flock together, but Eagles fly above the rest!

**Chapter 4 Leveraging Relationships Question #4:** How much time did you spend networking yourself today?

**Answer:** Not Enough!

**Action Item That Works #10:** Create perceived value!

> **Don't #1:** Don't abuse your referrals!

**Action Item That Works #11:** Communicate!

> **Don't #2:** Don't be afraid to ask!

**Action Item That Works #12:** Be Firm!

> **Don't #3:** Don't forget to give back!

**Salesology Principle #4:** If you think you can, or think you can't, you're right!

**Chapter 5 Sells vs. Sales Question #4:** What did you take away from this book?

**Answer:** There is No Excuse!

**Action Item That Works #13:** Understand personality!

> **Don't #1:** Don't let sales determine a relationship!

**Action Item That Works #14:** Send positive press!

> **Don't #2:** Don't just sell for today!

**<u>Action Item That Works #15:</u>**  Always be prospecting!

**<u>Don't #3:</u>**  Don't be mistaken!

**<u>Salesology Principle #5:</u>**  Make selling win/win!

# *Bonus Notes from Robert*

## NO EXCUSE! SELLING

**The Principles Accountability** = *No Excuse Principle #1-* If you do well or if you do bad, you reap what you sow. Take personal responsibility and hold yourself to a higher accountability.

**Smarter** = *No Excuse Principle #2* The early bird gets the worm but the 2nd mouse gets the cheese - think smarter, work smarter.

**Consistency** = *No Excuse Principle #3* birds of a feather, flock together, eagles fly above the rest - the value you bring determines your reputation.

**Motivation** = *No Excuse Principle #4* If you think you can or think you can't, you're right. You are what you think, dare to be more!

**Passion** = *No Excuse Principle #5* Money and People follow Passion, not the other way around. You do well what you love.

## The Keys
-Be careful what you spend your time on
-Find the valuable
-Go with your passion
-Grow yourself, train yourself
-Plan from End to Beginning

## No Excuse!
This is not an introduction, it's our Creed:  No Excuse is a mindset. You are what you think. To accept responsibility, is to achieve understanding, to move forward, to arrive at No Excuse.  The pressure to produce is a fact, but to accept it is to turn it to your advantage.  It is about what you do, not what you didn't do.  Turn Iron into Gold.  Accept No Excuse!, Start today, Right Here, Right Now.

The **FIVE BASICS** of the **NO EXCUSE!** Mindset:

1 **BE TRAINED** by mentors, training courses, and self-improvement
2 **BE ORGANIZED** using time management, social media, computers, iPhones
3 **BRING VALUE** real value
4 **BRING PASSION** this in NOT an 8-5 job
5 **BUILD RELATIONSHIPS INVEST** in people

**No Excuse! Selling** is a mindset. You don't have to be the top salesperson in the world, you certainly don't want to be the worst, but you have to see the profession for what it is, influencing and guiding someone to make a decision and getting resolution. Your effectiveness rests on that.  You knew what the job was about    when you took it so get trained and get professional, blame no one but yourself, turn iron into gold, but in the end stop right now realize that your career is what you make it, you are responsible. Start today, right here, right not.

-Stick to the basics, it sounds simple but following the basics will create sustainable sales.  It's easy to lazy but success doesn't work on your time.
-If you're the last to know, you're the first to go!
-Let hard work dictate your value.

-Either you're 100% on the team or find a new team, because if you stay you will destroy the team.

No excuses, find another sandbox to play in. Either get on the boat or be left behind. You can't have one foot on the dock and one on the boat.

Get on or get off! You're part of the solution or you're part of the problem.

## **IT STARTS WITH NO EXCUSE! SELLING**

www.ingramcontent.com/pod-product-compliance
Lightning Source LLC
Chambersburg PA
CBHW020512100426
42813CB00030B/3212/J